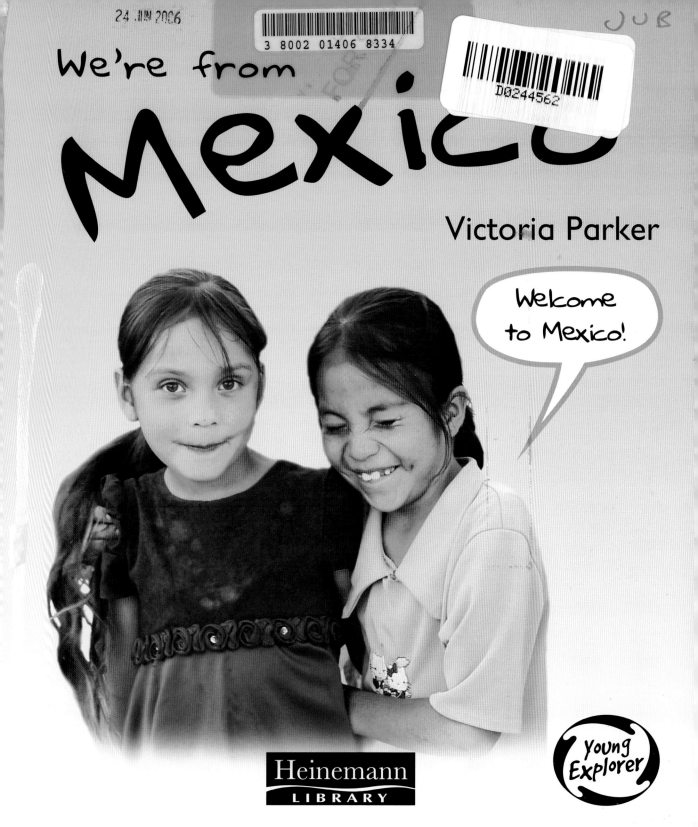

We're from
Mexico

Victoria Parker

Welcome to Mexico!

Heinemann
LIBRARY

Young Explorer

H www.heinemann.co.uk/library

Visit our website to find out more information about **Heinemann Library** books.

To order:
☎ Phone 44 (0) 1865 888066
▤ Send a fax to 44 (0) 1865 314091
▣ Visit the Heinemann Bookshop at www.heinemann.co.uk/library to browse our catalogue and order online.

First published in Great Britain by Heinemann Library, Halley Court, Jordan Hill, Oxford OX2 8EJ, part of Harcourt Education.
Heinemann is a registered trademark of Harcourt Education Ltd.

Editorial: Jilly Attwood and Kate Bellamy
Design: Ron Kamen and Celia Jones
Photographer: John Millar
Picture Research: Maria Joannou
Production: Séverine Ribierre

Originated by Ambassador Litho Ltd
Printed and bound in China by South China Printing Company

ISBN 0 431 11934 1 (hardback)
09 08 07 06 05
10 9 8 7 6 5 4 3 2 1

ISBN 0 431 11941 4 (paperback)
10 09 08 07 06
10 9 8 7 6 5 4 3 2 1

British Library Cataloguing in Publication Data

Parker, Victoria
We're From Mexico
972'.0841

A full catalogue record for this book is available from the British Library.

Acknowledgements

Corbis/Royalty Free pp. **4a**, **4b**, **30c**; John Millar pp. **1**, **5a**, **5b**, **5c**, **6**, **7a**, **7b**, **8**, **9**, **10a**, **11**, **12**, **13**, **14** ,**15**, **16** ,**17a**, **17b**, **18a**, **18b**, **19**, **20**, **21a**, **21b**, **22**, **23**, **24**, **25a**, **25b**, **26**, **27a**, **27b**, **28**, **29a**, **29b**, **30a**, **30b**

Cover photograph of Mexican school girls, reproduced with permission of John Millar.

Many thanks to Nayeli, Luis, Raul and their families.

Every effort has been made to contact copyright holders of any material reproduced in this book. Any omissions will be rectified in subsequent printings if notice is given to the publishers.

The paper used to print this book comes from sustainable resources.

Contents

Words appearing in the text in bold, **like this**, are explained in the Glossary.

 Find out more about Mexico at www.heinemannexplore.co.uk

Where is Mexico?

To learn about Mexico we meet three children who live there. Mexico is a very large country. It is south of the United States.

▲ This is a map of Mexico. The capital of Mexico is Mexico City.

◀ Mexico has many mountains.

There are hot wet **rainforests** in south Mexico. ▶

◀ There are hot, dry **deserts** in north Mexico.

5

Meet Nayeli

Nayeli is eight years old. She comes from Mexico City, the capital of Mexico. She lives with her parents, her twin brother Abraham, and her two dogs – Gigo and Toby.

Nayeli

Abraham

Nayeli's father works in an office. He also owns three taxis. The family live in a big house with Nayeli's aunt, uncle and baby cousin.

Nayeli's parents

Nayeli's house ▶ has five bedrooms and a yard.

Nayeli at school

Nayeli enjoys school. She likes her uniform and her brightly painted classroom. She wants to be a teacher when she grows up.

▲ There are 48 children in Nayeli's class.

School starts at nine and finishes at two. Nayeli and her friends have a half hour break for lunch.

▲ Nayeli likes jam sandwiches, fruit, ice cream and cola.

Nayeli's home life

After school, Nayeli and her friend Abigail do their homework. Then they play basketball, go to the park or watch a film.

Abigail

At weekends, Nayeli does jobs at home for her mother. She likes to help with the cooking.

▲ Nayeli cooks breakfast for her family.

The people and the land

Mexico City is the biggest city in the world. It is on a high **plain** in the middle of Mexico. This is where most Mexicans live.

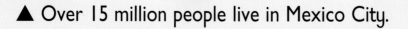

▲ Over 15 million people live in Mexico City.

Mexico has many **volcanoes**.
Sometimes they **erupt**. Earthquakes
and hurricanes can happen too. These
damage the land and people's homes.

13

Meet Luis

Luis is six years old. He comes from Huejuqilla. Huejuqilla is a small village in the mountains. He lives with his mother, two grandmothers, and his older brother and sister.

Luis's mother

Luis's grandmothers

Luis

There are not many jobs where Luis lives. So, Luis's father has gone to work in the United States. He comes home at Easter and Christmas.

▲ The main type of work around Luis's village is **cattle ranching**.

Luis's home

Luis lives in a small house with two bedrooms. In the little kitchen, Luis's mother cooks food. She sells it in the school shop.

▲ Luis and his sister, Yensenia, like helping in the kitchen.

In their yard, Luis's family grow plants
and have a sink for washing. They
keep their pets here too. They have
three cats, two dogs and a pigeon!

Luis's day

Every morning, it is Luis's job to tidy the house and sweep the yard. Then he plays with his toy cars or his football.

▲ There are 19 children in Luis's class. They do
not wear school uniform.

In the afternoon, Luis goes to school.
Sometimes his class watch television
programmes of lessons that are made
in Mexico City.

Sundays in Mexico

On Sundays, most people in Mexico put on their best clothes and go to church.

Afterwards, they often do something fun.
They might go out for a meal . . .

...or walk in a park . . .

...or take a special trip.

Meet Raul

Raul is eight years old. He comes from a seaside village in Yucatan. Raul lives with his parents and his older brother and sister.

▲ Yucatan is very hot. People sleep in **hammocks** because they are cooler than beds.

Raul's home is all on one level. It has three bedrooms, a living room, a dining room, a kitchen and a shower room.

Gone fishing

Every family in Raul's village owns a boat. Raul's father takes his boat out each day to go fishing. At weekends, Raul helps him.

▲ Raul is learning how to be a fisherman like his dad.

Raul's father sells most of the fish he catches. But he brings some home for the family to eat too.

Raul's daily jobs

On weekdays, Raul goes to school from seven until twelve o'clock. In the afternoons, he does a job. He cycles around selling cakes for the village bakery.

On Sundays, Raul helps at church as an **altar boy**. He prays for help with his lessons and for his father to catch lots of fish.

▲ Raul spends his spare time with his guitar and his pets.

Mexico's history

People have lived in Mexico for thousands of years. Long ago these included the Toltecs, Maya and Aztecs. They built huge stone cities that you can still visit today.

▲ The Maya built this **temple** in a city called Chichen Itza.

About 500 years ago, Spanish people arrived in Mexico. They took charge of the country for 300 years. Today the main language of Mexico is a type of Spanish.

▲ Spanish people made ▶ made many buildings in Mexico City.

Mexican fact file

Flag   **Capital city**   **Money**

Mexico City

Peso

Religion
- Most people in Mexico are Roman Catholic Christians.

Language
- The main language is Mexican Spanish. There are over 50 other languages spoken in different parts of the country.

Try speaking Mexican Spanish!
hola .... hello
que pasa? .... how are you?
gracias .... thank you

 Find out more about Mexico at
www.heinemannexplore.co.uk

Glossary

altar boy boy who helps in church

cattle ranching job of herding cows over a huge area of land

desert very hot, dry area of land that has almost no rain and very few plants

erupt to burst out of

hammock net that hangs off the floor for people to lie in

plain large, flat, grassy area of land with few trees

rainforest thick forest of tall trees that grow in a hot, rainy place

temple where people go to pray

volcano mountain that has a hole down into the Earth. Sometimes melted rock and ash erupt from it.

More books to read

Around the World: Schools, Margaret Hall (Heinemann Library, 2002)

Continents: South American, Leila Foster and Mary Fox (Heinemann Library, 2002)

Index